salads

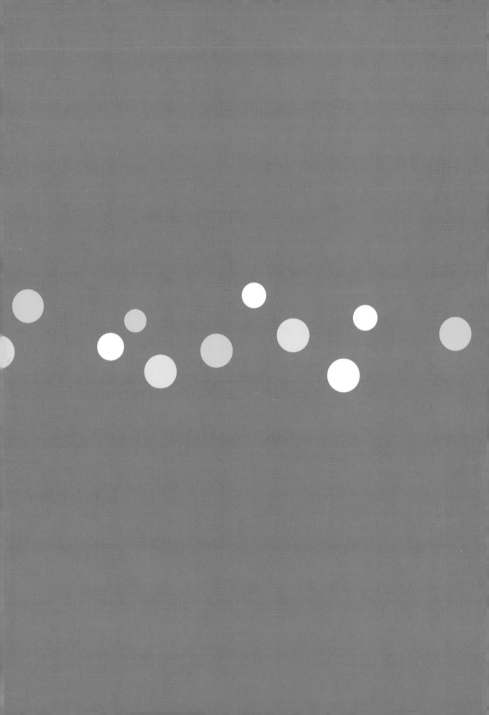

salads

MURDOCH BOOKS

contents

tossed

The acclaimed French chef Alexis Soyer hypothetically asked if there were anything 'more refreshing than salads when your appetite seems to have deserted you?'.

Cooks and diners have embraced a veritable world of salads bursting with bright, tangy flavours, wondrous textures and an array of fresh ingredients. Of course we all still love the classics — potato salad, bean salad, and coleslaw, for example. But it's been nothing short of a gastronomic epiphany to delve into the vegetable crisper, the deli, and other cuisines, to realise that salad combinations such as orange, goat's cheese and hazelnut or watercress, feta and watermelon are delicious possibilities.

We've taken cues from Morocco and tossed carrots with olives and mint, and from Thailand we have slippery noodle salads. Salad boredom is forever banished with the chargrilling of cauliflower, the roasting of tomatoes and the serving of potato salad warm, slathered in a tasty green olive dressing.

Salads can be light, complementing a main course or they can serve as an appetite-teasing starter. Salads can also be substantial meals in their own right, based around generous serves of meat, tofu or seafood. They can be dressed with the simplest slick of oil and vinegar, homemade mayonnaise or special vinaigrettes. Whether humble and homey, sophisticated, comforting and familiar or thrillingly foreign, there's a salad recipe here for any and every occasion you could possibly imagine.

classic

Caesar salad

3 eggs
3 garlic cloves, crushed
2–3 anchovy fillets
1 teaspoon worcestershire sauce
2 tablespoons lime juice
1 teaspoon dijon mustard
185 ml (6 fl oz/¾ cup) olive oil
3 slices white bread
20 g (¾ oz/½ oz) butter
1 tablespoon olive oil, extra
3 bacon slices
1 large or 4 baby cos (romaine) lettuces
75 g (3¼ oz/¾ cup) shaved parmesan cheese

Process the eggs, garlic, anchovies, worcestershire sauce, lime juice and mustard in a food processor until smooth. With the motor running, add the oil in a thin, continuous stream to produce a creamy dressing. Season to taste.

Cut the crusts off the bread, then cut the bread into 1.5 cm (⅝ inch) cubes.

Heat the butter and extra olive oil in a frying pan over medium heat. Add the bread and cook for 5–8 minutes, or until crisp, then remove from the pan. Cook the bacon in the pan for 3 minutes, or until crisp, then break into bite-sized pieces.

Toss the lettuce leaves with the dressing, then add the croutons and bacon and top with the parmesan cheese.

SERVES 4–6

Green salad with lemon vinaigrette

150 g (5½ oz) baby cos (romaine) lettuce
150 g (5½ oz) small butter lettuce
50 g (1¾ oz) watercress
100 g (3½ oz) rocket (arugula)
1 tablespoon finely chopped French shallots
2 teaspoons dijon mustard
½ teaspoon sugar
1 tablespoon finely chopped basil
1 teaspoon grated lemon zest
3 teaspoons lemon juice
1 tablespoon white wine vinegar
25 ml (1 fl oz) lemon oil
75 ml (2½ fl oz) virgin olive oil

Remove the outer leaves from the cos and butter lettuces and separate the core leaves. Wash in cold water, place in a colander to drain, then refrigerate. Pinch or trim the stalks from the watercress and rocket,. Pat dry and chill with the lettuce.

To make the dressing, whisk together the shallots, mustard, sugar, basil, lemon zest, lemon juice and vinegar in a bowl until well blended. Place the oils in a small jug and slowly add to the bowl in a thin stream, whisking constantly to create a smooth, creamy dressing. Season to taste.

Put the salad greens in a large bowl. Drizzle the dressing over the salad and toss gently to coat.

SERVES 6

Panzanella

200 g (7 oz) ciabatta bread
8 vine-ripened tomatoes
4 tablespoons olive oil
1 tablespoon lemon juice
1½ tablespoons red wine vinegar
6 anchovy fillets, finely chopped
1 tablespoon baby capers, rinsed, drained and finely chopped
1 garlic clove, crushed
30 g (1 oz) basil leaves

Preheat the oven to 220°C (425°F/ Gas 7). Tear the bread into 2 cm (¾ inch) pieces. Spread on a baking tray and bake for 5–7 minutes, or until golden. Leave the toasted bread on a wire rack to cool.

Score a cross in the base of each tomato. Place in a heatproof bowl and cover with boiling water. Leave for 30 seconds, then transfer to cold water and peel the skin away from the cross. Cut four of the tomatoes in half and squeeze the juice and seeds into a bowl, reserving and chopping the flesh. Add the oil, juice, vinegar, anchovies, capers and garlic to the tomato juice and season.

Seed and slice the remaining tomatoes, and place in a large bowl with the reserved tomato and most of the basil. Add the dressing and toasted bread, and toss. Garnish with the remaining basil, season, and leave for at least 15 minutes. Serve at room temperature.

NOTE: This salad is also known as Tuscan bread salad.

Greek salad

4 tomatoes, cut into wedges
1 telegraph (long) cucumber, peeled, halved,
    seeded and cut into small cubes
2 green capsicums (pepper), seeded, halved
    lengthways and cut into strips
1 red onion, finely sliced
16 Kalamata olives
250 g (9 oz) firm feta cheese, cut into cubes
1 small handful flat-leaf (Italian) parsley
12 mint leaves
125 ml (4 fl oz/½ cup) olive oil
2 tablespoons lemon juice
1 garlic clove, crushed

Put the tomato, cucumber, capsicum, onion, olives, feta and half the parsley and mint leaves in a large salad bowl and gently mix together.

Put the oil, juice and garlic in a screwtop jar, season and shake until combined. Pour the dressing over the salad and toss lightly. Garnish with the remaining parsley and mint.

SERVES 4

Coleslaw

½ green cabbage
¼ red cabbage
3 carrots, coarsely grated
6 radishes, coarsely grated
1 red capsicum (pepper), chopped
4 spring onions (scallions), sliced
15 g (¼ oz) chopped flat-leaf (italian) parsley
250 g (9 oz/1 cup) whole-egg mayonnaise

Remove the hard core from the cabbages and shred the leaves with a sharp knife. Put in a large bowl and add the carrot, radish, capsicum, spring onion and parsley to the bowl.

Add the mayonnaise, season to taste and toss until well combined.

SERVES 8–10

NOTE: Cover and refrigerate the chopped vegetables for up to 3 hours before serving. Add the mayonnaise just before serving.

Dill potato salad

600 g (1 lb 5 oz) desiree potatoes
2 eggs
2 tablespoons finely chopped dill
1½ tablespoons finely chopped French shallots
1 egg yolk
2 teaspoons lemon juice
1 teaspoon dijon mustard
100 ml (3½ fl oz) light olive oil

Bring a large saucepan of water to the boil. Cook the potatoes for 20 minutes, or until tender. Add the eggs for the last 10 minutes. Remove the potatoes and eggs, and allow to cool.

Peel the potatoes, then cut into 2–3 cm (³⁄₄–1¼ inch) cubes. Peel and chop the eggs. Place the potatoes in a large bowl with the dill, eggs and shallots. Toss to combine, then season.

Process the egg yolk, lemon juice, mustard and a pinch of salt in a food processor. With the motor running, gradually add the olive oil a few drops at a time. When about half the oil has been added, pour in the remaining oil in a steady stream until it has all been incorporated. Use a large metal spoon to gently combine the potato and mayonnaise, then serve.

SERVES 4

Salad Niçoise

3 tablespoons lemon juice
1 garlic clove, crushed
140 ml (5 fl oz) olive oil
400 g (14 oz) waxy potatoes,
   such as Charlotte or Kipfler
3 eggs
120 g (4 oz) green beans,
   trimmed
1 green capsicum (pepper),
   seeded and sliced

120 g (4 oz) black olives
300 g (10½ oz) firm, ripe
   tomatoes, cut into wedges
100 g (3½ oz) Lebanese (short)
   cucumber, cut into chunks
3 spring onions (scallions), cut
   into 2 cm (¾ inch) pieces
600 g (1 lb 5 oz) fresh tuna
   steaks

Put the lemon juice, garlic and 120 ml (4 fl oz) of olive oil in a jar with a screw-top lid. Season and shake the jar well to combine.

Boil the potatoes in a saucepan of salted water for 10–12 minutes, or until tender. Add the eggs for the final 8 minutes of cooking. Drain, cool the eggs under cold water, then peel and quarter. Cool the potatoes, then cut into chunks. Bring a saucepan of salted water to the boil, add the green beans and blanch for 3 minutes. Drain and refresh under cold water. Drain well, then slice in half on the diagonal.

Put the potato and beans in a large bowl, and add the capsicum, olives, tomatoes, cucumber and spring onion. Strain the garlic from the dressing. Pour half over the salad, toss and transfer to a serving dish.

Heat a frying pan over very high heat. Add the remaining olive oil. Season the tuna steaks and cook for 2 minutes on each side, or until rare. Allow to cool for 5 minutes, then slice thinly. Arrange on top of the salad with the eggs, and drizzle with the remaining dressing.

SERVES 4

Egg salad with creamy dressing

10 large eggs, at room
   temperature
1 egg yolk
3 teaspoons lemon juice
2 teaspoons dijon mustard
70 ml (2½ fl oz) olive oil
70 ml (2½ fl oz) safflower oil

2 tablespoons chopped dill
30 ml (1 fl oz) crème fraîche or
   sour cream
2 tablespoons baby capers,
   rinsed and drained
20 g (¾ oz) mustard cress

Put the eggs in a large saucepan of cold water. Bring to the boil and simmer gently for 10 minutes. Drain, then cool the eggs under cold running water. Remove the shells.

Place the egg yolk, lemon juice and dijon mustard in a food processor or blender and season. With the motor running, slowly add the combined olive oil and safflower oil, drop by drop at first, then slowly increasing the amount to a thin, steady stream as the mixture thickens. When all of the oil has been added, put the mayonnaise in a large bowl and gently stir in the dill, crème fraîche and capers.

Roughly chop the eggs and fold into the mayonnaise. Transfer the salad to a serving bowl and use scissors to cut the green tips from the mustard cress. Scatter over the salad and serve.

SERVES 4

Tabbouleh

130 g (4¾ oz/¾ cup) burghul (bulgur)
3 ripe tomatoes
1 telegraph (long) cucumber
4 spring onions (scallions), sliced
120 g (4 oz) chopped flat-leaf (Italian) parsley
25 g (1 oz) chopped mint

Dressing
4 tablespoons lemon juice
3 tablespoons olive oil
1 tablespoon extra virgin olive oil

Place the burghul in a bowl, cover with 500 ml (17 fl oz/2 cups) of water and leave for 1½ hours.

Cut the tomatoes in half, squeeze to remove any excess seeds and cut into 1 cm (½ inch) cubes. Cut the cucumber in half lengthways, remove the seeds with a teaspoon and cut the flesh into 1 cm (½ inch) cubes.

To make the dressing, place the lemon juice and 1½ teaspoons salt in a bowl and whisk until well combined. Season well with freshly ground black pepper and slowly whisk in the olive oil and extra virgin olive oil.

Drain the burghul and squeeze out any excess water. Spread the burghul out on paper towels and leave to dry for about 30 minutes. Put the burghul in a large salad bowl, add the tomato, cucumber, spring onion, parsley and mint, and toss well to combine. Pour the dressing over the salad and toss until evenly coated.

SERVES 6

Fattoush

2 pitta bread rounds
6 cos (romaine) lettuce leaves, shredded
1 large Lebanese (short) cucumber, cubed
4 tomatoes, cut into 1 cm (¾ inch) cubes
8 spring onions (scallions), chopped
4 tablespoons finely chopped flat-leaf (Italian) parsley
1 tablespoon finely chopped mint
2 tablespoons finely chopped coriander (cilantro)

Dressing
2 garlic cloves, crushed
100 ml (3½ oz) extra virgin olive oil
100 ml (3½ oz) lemon juice

Preheat the oven to 180°C (350°F/Gas 4). Split the bread in half through the centre and bake on a baking tray for 8–10 minutes, or until golden and crisp, turning halfway through. Break into pieces.

To make the dressing, whisk all the ingredients together in a bowl until well combined.

Place the bread and remaining salad ingredients in a serving bowl and toss to combine. Drizzle with the dressing and toss well. Season to taste. Serve immediately.

SERVES 6

Insalata caprese

3 large vine-ripened tomatoes
250 g (9 oz) bocconcini (fresh baby mozzarella cheese)
12 basil leaves
3 tablespoons extra virgin olive oil
4 basil leaves, extra, roughly torn

Slice the tomato into twelve 1 cm (½ inch) slices. Slice the bocconcini into 24 slices the same thickness as the tomato.

Arrange the tomato slices on a plate, alternating them with 2 slices of bocconcini and placing a basil leaf between the bocconcini slices.

Drizzle with the olive oil, sprinkle with the torn basil and season well.

SERVES 4

starters

Chargrilled vegetable salad

4 baby eggplants (aubergine)
5 Roma (plum) tomatoes
2 red capsicums (peppers)
1 green capsicum (pepper)
2 zucchini (courgettes)
100 ml (3½ fl oz) olive oil
12 baby bocconcini (fresh baby mozarella cheese)
45 g (1½ oz/¼ cup) Ligurian olives
1 garlic clove, finely chopped
3 teaspoons baby capers
½ teaspoon sugar
2 tablespoons balsamic vinegar

Cut the eggplants and tomatoes in half lengthways. Cut the red and green capsicums in half lengthways, remove the seeds and membrane then cut each half into 3 pieces. Thinly slice the zucchini on the diagonal.

Preheat a chargrill pan over medium heat. Add 1 tablespoon of oil and cook a quarter of the vegetables (cook the tomatoes cut-side down first) for about 2–3 minutes, or until marked and golden. Put in a bowl.

Cook the remaining vegetables in batches until tender, adding more oil as needed. Transfer to the bowl and add the baby bocconcini. Mix the olives, garlic, capers, sugar, vinegar and remaining oil (about 2 tablespoons). Pour over the salad and toss. Season with pepper.

SERVES 4–6

Asparagus orange salad

300 g (10½ oz) thin asparagus spears
50 g (1¾ oz) watercress
½ small red onion, very thinly sliced
1 orange, cut into 12 segments
1 tablespoon fresh orange juice
1 teaspoon finely grated orange zest
1 teaspoon sugar
1 tablespoon red wine vinegar
2 teaspoons poppy seeds
2 tablespoons olive oil
60 g (2¼ oz) soft goat's cheese

Cook the asparagus in boiling water for 1–2 minutes, or until just tender. Rinse under cold water to cool.

Combine the asparagus with the watercress, red onion and orange segments on a serving platter.

Combine the orange juice, orange zest, sugar, red wine vinegar and poppy seeds in a cup. Whisk in the oil with a fork until combined and drizzle over the salad. Crumble the goat's cheese over the salad and season to taste.

SERVES 4

Frisée and garlic crouton salad

Vinaigrette
1 French shallot, finely chopped
1 tablespoon dijon mustard
3 tablespoons tarragon vinegar
170 ml (6 fl oz/²⁄₃ cup) extra virgin olive oil

1 tablespoon olive oil
½ bread stick, sliced
4 whole garlic cloves
1 baby frisée (curly endive), washed and dried
100 g (3½ oz) walnuts, toasted
100 g (3½ oz) feta cheese, crumbled

To make the vinaigrette, whisk together the shallot, mustard and vinegar in a bowl. Slowly add the oil, whisking constantly until thickened. Set aside.

Heat the oil in a large frying pan over medium–high heat. Add the bread and garlic cloves and cook for 5–8 minutes, or until the croutons are crisp. Remove the garlic from the pan. Once the croutons are cool, break into small pieces.

Place the frisée, croutons, walnuts, feta cheese and vinaigrette in a large bowl. Toss together well and serve.

SERVES 4–6

Bacon and avocado salad

8 bacon slices
400 g (14 oz) green beans, topped, tailed and halved
300 g (10½ oz) baby English spinach leaves
2 French shallots, finely sliced
2 avocados
¼ teaspoon brown sugar
1 garlic clove, crushed
4 tablespoons olive oil
1 tablespoon balsamic vinegar
1 teaspoon sesame oil

Preheat the grill (broiler). Put the bacon on a tray and grill (broil) on both sides until crisp. Leave to cool, then break into pieces.

Bring a saucepan of water to the boil and cook the beans for 4 minutes. Drain and rinse under cold running water for a few seconds.

Put the spinach in a large bowl and add the beans, bacon and shallots. Halve the avocados, then cut into cubes and add to the bowl.

Mix the brown sugar and garlic in a small bowl. Add the remaining ingredients and whisk together.

Pour the dressing over the salad and toss well. Season before serving.

SERVES 4

Smoked salmon and rocket salad

Dressing
2 tablespoons extra virgin olive oil
1 tablespoon balsamic vinegar

150 g (5½ oz) rocket (arugula) leaves
1 avocado
250 g (9 oz) smoked salmon slices
325 g (11½ oz) marinated goat's cheese, drained and crumbled
2 tablespoons roasted hazelnuts, roughly chopped

Fish substitution
smoked trout

To make the dressing, thoroughly whisk together the oil and vinegar in a bowl. Season to taste.

Trim the long stems from the rocket. Rinse the leaves, pat dry and gently toss in a bowl with the dressing.

Cut the avocado into wedges. Put about three wedges on each serving plate with the salmon and rocket. Scatter the cheese and nuts over the top and season with freshly ground black pepper.

SERVES 4

Broad bean, mint and bacon salad

600 g (1 lb 5 oz) frozen broad (fava) beans (see Notes)
150 g (5½ oz) shredded butter or cos (romaine) lettuce
35 g (1¼ oz) shredded mint
250 g (9 oz) Kasseler or pancetta (see Notes)
1 tablespoon olive oil

1½ teaspoons dijon mustard
1 teaspoon sugar
2 tablespoons white wine vinegar
3 tablespoons extra virgin olive oil
4 flatbreads

Blanch the beans, according to packet instructions. Drain, rinse under cold water, and peel. Place in a large bowl with the lettuce and mint.

Slice the Kasseler into thick slices, then into 2 cm (¾ inch) chunks. Heat the oil in a heavy-based frying pan and cook the Kasseler for 3–4 minutes, or until golden. Add to the bean mixture.

Combine the mustard, sugar and vinegar in a cup. Whisk in the extra virgin oil until well combined and season. Pile the salad onto fresh or lightly toasted flatbreads to serve.

SERVES 4

NOTES: If they are in season, you may like to use fresh broad beans. You will need about 1.8 kg (4 lb) of beans in the pod to give 600 g (1 lb 5 oz) of beans. Boil the beans for 2 minutes and peel before using them.

Kasseler is a traditional German speciality. It is a cured and smoked loin of pork that comes in a single piece and should be available at good delicatessens.

Avocado and grapefruit salad

2 ruby grapefruit
1 ripe avocado
200 g (7 oz) watercress leaves
1 French shallot, finely sliced
1 tablespoon sherry vinegar
3 tablespoons olive oil

Peel and segment the grapefruit, working over a bowl to save any juice drips for the dressing.

Cut the avocado into 2 cm (¾ inch) wedges and put in a bowl with the watercress, grapefruit and shallot.

Put 1 tablespoon of the reserved grapefruit juice in a small, screw-top jar with the sherry vinegar, olive oil, salt and black pepper, and shake well. Pour the dressing over the salad and toss gently.

SERVES 4

Orange and goat's cheese salad

20 g (¾ oz) hazelnuts
1 tablespoon orange juice
1 tablespoon lemon juice
125 ml (4 fl oz/½ cup) olive oil
250 g (9 oz) watercress, well
    rinsed and dried

50 g (1¾ oz) baby English
    spinach leaves, well rinsed
    and dried
24 orange segments
300 g (10½ oz) firm goat's
    cheese, sliced into 4 equal
    portions

Preheat the oven to 180°C (350°F/ Gas 4). Put the hazelnuts on a tray and roast for 5–6 minutes, or until the skin turns dark brown. Wrap the hazelnuts in a dish cloth and rub together to remove the skins.

Combine the nuts, orange juice, lemon juice and a pinch of salt in a food processor. With the motor running, gradually add the oil a few drops at a time. When about half the oil has been added, pour in the remainder in a steady stream.

Remove the stems from the watercress and put the leaves in a bowl with the spinach, orange segments and 2 tablespoons of the dressing. Toss to combine and season to taste with pepper. Arrange the salad on four plates.

Heat a small, non-stick frying pan over medium–high heat and brush lightly with olive oil. When hot, carefully press each slice of goat's cheese firmly into the pan and cook for 1–2 minutes, or until a crust has formed on the cheese. Carefully remove the cheese from the pan and arrange over the salads, crust-side-up. Drizzle the remaining dressing over the salads.

SERVES 4

Pear and walnut salad

Dressing
100 g (3½ oz) creamy blue
  cheese
3 tablespoons olive oil
1 tablespoon walnut oil
1 tablespoon lemon juice
1 tablespoon cream
2 teaspoons finely chopped sage

100 g (3½ oz/1 cup) walnut
  halves
4 firm, ripe small pears
2 tablespoons lemon juice
2 heads witlof (chicory/Belgian
  endive), trimmed and leaves
  separated
100 g (3½ oz/1 cup) parmesan
  cheese, shaved

To make the dressing, purée the blue cheese in a small processor, then add the olive oil, walnut oil and lemon juice, and blend until smooth. With the motor running, slowly add 2 teaspoons of warm water. Stir in the cream and sage and season to taste.

Preheat the grill (broiler). Put the walnuts in a bowl and cover with boiling water. Allow to soak for 1 minute, then drain. Spread the walnuts on a baking tray and place under the grill for 3 minutes, or until lightly toasted. Chop coarsely.

Thinly slice across the pears through the core to make rounds. Do not peel or core the pears, but discard the seeds. As each pear is sliced, sprinkle with a little lemon juice to prevent discoloration. On each serving plate, arrange three pear slices in a circle. Top with a scattering of walnuts, a couple of endive leaves, a few more walnuts and some parmesan. Repeat this layering, reserving the last layer of parmesan and some of the walnuts. Spoon some dressing over each stack, scatter with the remaining walnuts, and top each with the reserved parmesan.

SERVES 4

Mixed salad with warm Brie dressing

½ sourdough baguette
165 ml (5½ fl oz) extra virgin
 olive oil
6 bacon slices
2 garlic cloves, peeled
2 baby cos (romaine) lettuce
90 g (3¼ oz) baby English
 spinach leaves

80 g (2¾ oz/½ cup) pine nuts,
 toasted
2 French shallots, finely
 chopped
1 tablespoon dijon mustard
4 tablespoons sherry vinegar
300 g (10½ oz) ripe Brie cheese,
 rind removed

Preheat the oven to 180°C (350°F/ Gas 4). Thinly slice the baguette on the diagonal. Use 2 tablespoons of oil to brush both sides of each slice, place on a baking tray and bake for 20 minutes, or until golden.

Place the bacon on a separate tray and bake for 3–5 minutes, or until crisp. Remove the bread from the oven and use one garlic clove, cut in half, to rub the bread slices. Break the bacon into pieces and leave to cool.

Remove the outer leaves of the cos lettuce. Rinse the inner leaves well, drain, dry and place in a large bowl with the spinach. Add the bacon, croutons and pine nuts.

Place the remaining olive oil in a frying pan and heat gently. Add the shallots and cook until they soften, then crush the remaining garlic clove and add to the pan. Whisk in the mustard and vinegar, then gently whisk in the chopped Brie until it has melted. Remove the dressing from the heat and, while it is still warm, pour over the salad and toss gently.

SERVES 4

Artichoke, prosciutto and rocket salad

4 artichokes
2 eggs, lightly beaten
20 g (¾ oz/¼ cup) fresh
    breadcrumbs
25 g (1 oz/¼ cup) grated
    parmesan cheese

olive oil for frying
8 slices prosciutto
3 teaspoons white wine vinegar
1 garlic clove, crushed
3 handfuls rocket (arugula),
    long stalks trimmed

Bring a large saucepan of water to a boil. Remove the hard, outer leaves of each artichoke, trim the stem and cut 2.5 cm (1 inch) off the top. Cut into quarters and remove the furry 'choke'. Boil the pieces for 2 minutes, then drain.

Whisk the eggs in a bowl and mix the seasoned bread crumbs and grated pparmesan in another bowl. Dip each artichoke quarter into the egg, then roll in the crumb mixture to coat. Fill a frying pan with olive oil to a depth of 2 cm (¾ inch) and heat over medium–high heat. Add the artichokes in batches and fry for 2–3 minutes, or until golden. Remove from the pan and drain on paper towels.

Heat 1 tablespoon of olive oil in a nonstick frying pan over medium–high heat. Cook the prosciutto in two batches for 2 minutes, or until crisp and golden. Remove from the pan, reserving the oil.

Combine the reserved oil, vinegar and garlic with a little salt and pepper. Place the arugula in a bowl, add half of the salad dressing and toss well. Divide the arugula, artichokes and prosciutto among four plates, and drizzle with the remaining dressing. Sprinkle with sea salt.

SERVES 4

Watercress, feta and watermelon salad

2 tablespoons sunflower seeds
475 g (1 lb 1 oz) rindless watermelon, cut into 1 cm (¾ inch) cubes
180 g (6 oz) feta cheese, cut into 1 cm (¾ inch) cubes
75 g (2½ oz) watercress sprigs
2 tablespoons olive oil
1 tablespoon lemon juice
2 teaspoons chopped oregano

Heat a small frying pan over high heat. Add the sunflower seeds and, shaking the pan continuously, dry-fry for 2 minutes, or until toasted and lightly golden.

Put the watermelon, feta and watercress leaves in a large serving dish and toss gently to combine.

Combine the olive oil, lemon juice and chopped oregano in a small cup and season to taste. Pour the dressing over the salad and toss together well. Scatter with the toasted sunflower seeds and serve.

SERVES 4

Mushroom and goat's cheese salad

Dressing
2 tablespoons lemon juice
3 tablespoons olive oil
1 teaspoon grated lemon zest

8 large cap mushrooms, stems removed
1 tablespoon chopped thyme

4 garlic cloves, finely chopped
2 tablespoons olive oil
50 g (1¾ oz) baby rocket (arugula)
100 g (3½ oz) goat's cheese
2 tablespoons chopped flat-leaf (Italian) parsley

Preheat the oven to 200°C (400°F/ Gas 6). To make the dressing, combine the juice, oil and zest in a small bowl.

Put the mushrooms on a large baking tray, sprinkle with thyme and garlic, then drizzle with olive oil. Cover with foil and roast for 20 minutes. Remove the mushrooms from the oven and toss to combine the flavours. Re-cover and roast for a further 10 minutes, or until cooked. Remove the mushrooms from the oven and cut in half.

Place the rocket on a serving platter, top with the mushrooms and crumble the goat's cheese over the top.

Whisk the dressing to ensure it is well combined and drizzle over the salad. Serve sprinkled with parsley.

SERVES 4–6

Haloumi and asparagus salad with salsa verde

225 g (8 oz) haloumi cheese
25 small, thin asparagus spears
2 tablespoons garlic oil
1 small handful basil leaves
1 small handful mint leaves
1 handful flat-leaf (Italian) parsley leaves
2 tablespoons baby capers, rinsed and drained
1 garlic clove
2 tablespoons olive oil
1 tablespoon lemon juice
1 tablespoon lime juice
2 handfuls mixed salad leaves (mesclun)

Heat a chargrill pan over medium heat. Cut the haloumi into 1 cm (½ inch) slices and cut each slice in half diagonally to make two small triangles. Brush the haloumi and asparagus with the garlic oil. Sear the asparagus for 1 minute or until just tender, and the haloumi until grill marks appear and it is warmed through. Keep warm.

To make the salsa verde, place the herbs, capers, garlic and oil in a food processor and blend until smooth. Add the juices, and pulse briefly.

Divide the salad leaves among four serving plates. Top with the haloumi and asparagus, and drizzle with a little salsa verde.

SERVES 4

Chicken Waldorf salad

750 ml (26 fl oz/3 cups) chicken stock
2 chicken breast fillets, skin removed
2 red apples
2 green apples
2 celery stalks, sliced
100 g (3½ oz) toasted walnuts
125 g (4½ oz/½ cup) whole-egg mayonnaise
60 g (2¼ oz/¼ cup) sour cream
½ teaspoon chopped tarragon
1 baby cos (romaine) lettuce

Bring the stock to the boil in a medium saucepan. Remove from the heat, add the chicken to the stock, then cover and allow to cool in the liquid for 10 minutes, by which time the chicken should be cooked.

Cut the apples into bite-sized pieces. Shred the chicken breasts and place in a large bowl with the apple, celery, walnuts, mayonnaise, sour cream and tarragon. Season and toss well to combine. Separate the lettuce leaves and arrange in a serving bowl. Pile the Waldorf salad over the lettuce and serve.

SERVES 4

Semi-dried tomato and baby spinach salad

2 quarters of preserved lemon
150 g (5½ oz) baby English spinach leaves
200 g (7 oz) semi-dried (sun-blushed) tomatoes, sliced
225 g (8 oz) marinated artichoke hearts, drained and sliced
85 g (3 oz/½ cup) small black olives
2 tablespoons lemon juice
3 tablespoons olive oil
1 large garlic clove, crushed

Remove and discard the pith and flesh from the preserved lemon. Wash the zest and thinly slice.

Put the spinach leaves in a bowl with the semi-dried tomatoes, artichoke hearts, black olives and the preserved lemon slices.

Put the lemon juice, olive oil and garlic in a bowl, season and mix well. Pour over the spinach mixture and toss to coat. Serve immediately.

SERVES 6

Grilled haloumi and roast vegetable salad

4 slender eggplants (aubergine), halved lengthways
1 red capsicum (pepper), halved, thickly sliced
4 small zucchini (courgettes), cut in half, halved lengthways
4 tablespoons olive oil
2 garlic cloves, crushed
200 g (7 oz) haloumi cheese, cut into 5 mm (¼ inch) thick slices
150 g (5½ oz) baby English spinach leaves, trimmed
1 tablespoon balsamic vinegar

Preheat the oven to 220°C (425°F/Gas 7). Put the vegetables in a large bowl, add 3 tablespoons of olive oil and the garlic, season and toss well to combine.

Put the vegetables in an ovenproof dish in a single layer. Roast for 20–30 minutes, or until tender and browned around the edges.

Meanwhile, lightly brush a chargrill or heavy-based frying pan with oil and cook the haloumi slices for 1–2 minutes each side.

Place the spinach leaves on four serving plates. Top with the roast vegetables and haloumi. Place the remaining oil in a small bowl, add the vinegar and whisk to combine, then pour over the vegetables and haloumi. Serve immediately, warm or at room temperature.

SERVES 4

NOTE: You can use any roasted vegetable, such as orange sweet potatoes, leeks and Roma (plum) tomatoes.

Scallops, ginger and spinach salad

300 g (10½ oz) scallops, without roe
100 g (3½ oz) baby English spinach leaves
1 small red capsicum (pepper), cut into very fine strips
50 g (1¾ oz) bean sprouts, trimmed
25 ml (1 fl oz) sake
1 tablespoon lime juice
2 teaspoons shaved palm sugar or light brown sugar
1 teaspoon fish sauce

Remove any membrane or hard white muscle from the scallops. Lightly brush a chargrill pan with oil. Cook the scallops in batches for 1 minute each side, or until cooked.

Divide the spinach, capsicum strips and bean sprouts among four plates. Arrange the scallops over the top.

To make the dressing, place the sake, lime juice, palm sugar and fish sauce in a small bowl and mix together well. Pour over the salad and serve immediately.

SERVES 4

Prawn and fennel salad

1.25 kg (2 lb 12 oz) raw large prawns (shrimp),
   peeled and deveined
1 large fennel bulb (400 g/14 oz), thinly sliced
300 g (10½ oz) watercress
2 tablespoons finely chopped chives
125 ml (4 fl oz/½ cup) extra virgin olive oil
3 tablespoons lemon juice
1 tablespoon dijon mustard
1 large garlic clove, finely chopped

Bring a saucepan of water to the boil. Add the prawns and simmer for 2 minutes, or until pink and are cooked through. Drain and leave to cool. Pat the prawns dry with paper towels and slice in half lengthways. Place in a large serving bowl.

Add the fennel, watercress and chives to the bowl and mix well.

To make the dressing, whisk the oil, lemon juice, mustard and garlic together until combined. Pour the dressing over the salad, season and toss gently. Arrange the salad on serving plates and serve immediately.

SERVES 4

Scallop salad with saffron dressing

pinch saffron threads
60 g (2¼ oz/¼ cup) mayonnaise
1½ tablespoons pouring (whipping) cream
1 teaspoon lemon juice
20 scallops with roe attached
30 g (1 oz) butter
1 tablespoon olive oil
3 handfuls mixed salad leaves (mesclun)
1 small handful chervil leaves

To make the dressing, place the saffron threads in a bowl and soak in 2 teaspoons of hot water for 10 minutes. Add the mayonnaise and mix well. Stir in the whipping cream, then the lemon juice. Refrigerate until needed.

Heat the butter and olive oil in a large frying pan over high heat and sear the scallops in small batches for 1 minute on each side.

Divide the mixed salad leaves and chervil among four serving plates, then top each with five scallops. Drizzle the dressing over the scallops and the salad leaves before serving.

SERVES 4

Octopus salad

650 g (1 lb 7 oz) baby octopus, cleaned
120 g (4 oz) mixed salad leaves
lemon wedges, to serve

Dressing
2 tablespoons lemon juice
100 ml (3½ fl oz) olive oil
1 garlic clove, thinly sliced
1 tablespoon chopped mint
1 tablespoon chopped flat-leaf (Italian) parsley
1 teaspoon dijon mustard
pinch of cayenne pepper

Bring a large saucepan of water to the boil and add the octopus. Simmer for about 8–10 minutes, or until the octopus are tender to the point of a knife.

Meanwhile, make a dressing by mixing together the lemon juice, olive oil, garlic, mint, parsley, mustard and cayenne pepper and season.

Drain the octopus well and put in a bowl. Pour the dressing over the top and cool for a few minutes before transferring to the fridge. Chill for at least 3 hours before serving on a bed of salad leaves. Drizzle a little of the dressing over the top and serve with lemon wedges.

SERVES 4

Squid salad

Dressing

2 large garlic cloves, crushed

2 teaspoons grated fresh ginger

3 small fresh red chillies, seeded and thinly sliced

2 tablespoons grated palm sugar or soft brown sugar

2 tablespoons fish sauce

2 tablespoons lime juice

½ teaspoon sesame oil

500 g (1 lb 2 oz) squid tubes, cleaned

6 makrut (kaffir lime) leaves

1 stem lemon grass, white part only, chopped

3–4 red Asian shallots, thinly sliced

1 Lebanese (short) cucumber, cut in half lengthways and thinly sliced

3 tablespoons chopped coriander (cilantro) leaves

1 small handful fresh mint

150 g (5½ oz) oakleaf or coral lettuce, leaves separated

fried red Asian shallot flakes, to garnish

To make the dressing, heat the garlic, ginger, chilli, palm sugar, fish sauce, lime juice, sesame oil and 1 tablespoon water in a saucepan over low heat.

Cut the squid in half lengthways. Clean and remove any quills. Score a criss-cross pattern on the inside of the squid. Cut the squid into 3 cm (1¼ inch) pieces.

Place the makrut leaves, lemon grass and 1.25 litres (44 fl oz/5 cups) of water in a saucepan and bring to the boil. Reduce the heat and simmer for 5 minutes. Add half the squid pieces and cook for 30 seconds, or until they begin to curl up. Remove and keep warm. Repeat with the remaining squid. Discard the lime leaves, lemon grass and liquid.

Put the squid, shallots, cucumber, coriander, mint, lettuce and dressing in a large bowl and toss together. Serve garnished with the shallot flakes.

SERVES 4

Crab salad with mango and coconut

2 garlic cloves, peeled
2 small red chillies
2 tablespoons dried shrimp
2 tablespoons fish sauce
3 tablespoons lime juice
3 teaspoons palm sugar or soft
brown sugar
30 g (1 oz/½ cup) shredded
coconut
300 g (10½ oz/1½ cups)
shredded green mango
1 small handful mint leaves
(torn if very big)

1 small handful coriander
(cilantro) leaves
3 makrut (kaffir lime) leaves,
shredded
2 teaspoons thinly shredded,
pickled ginger
500 g (1 lb 2 oz) fresh crab meat

banana leaves, crushed toasted
peanuts and lime wedges,
to serve (optional)

Preheat the oven to 180°C (350°F/ Gas 4). Put the garlic, chillies, dried shrimp and ½ teaspoon salt in a mortar and pestle. Pound to a paste, then whisk in the fish sauce, lime juice and palm sugar with a fork.

Put the shredded coconut on a baking tray and bake for 3–5 minutes, shaking the tray occasionally to ensure even toasting. Watch the coconut closely, as it will burn easily.

Put the shredded mango in a large bowl and add the mint, coriander, makrut lime leaves, ginger, coconut and crabmeat. Pour on the dressing and toss together gently.

Place a piece of banana leaf (if using) in each serving bowl. Top with crab salad, sprinkle with the peanuts and serve immediately with lime wedges.

SERVES 4–6

Somen noodle salad

Sesame dressing
40 g (1½ oz/¼ cup) sesame
seeds, toasted
2½ tablespoons shoyu or light
soy sauce
2 tablespoons rice vinegar
2 teaspoons sugar
½ teaspoon grated fresh ginger
½ teaspoon dashi granules

125 g (4½ oz) dried somen
noodles

100 g (3½ oz) snow peas
(mangetout), finely sliced on
the diagonal
100 g (3½ oz) daikon radish,
julienned
100 g (3½ oz) carrot, julienned
1 spring onion (scallion), sliced
on the diagonal
50 g (1¾ oz) baby English
spinach leaves, trimmed
2 teaspoons toasted sesame
seeds

To make the dressing, place the sesame seeds in a mortar and pestle and grind until fine and moist. Combine the soy sauce, rice vinegar, sugar, ginger, dashi granules and 125 ml (4 fl oz/½ cup) of water in a saucepan and bring to the boil over high heat. Reduce the heat to medium and simmer, stirring, for 2 minutes, or until the dashi granules have dissolved. Remove from the heat. Cool. Gradually combine with the ground sesame seeds, stirring to form a thick dressing.

Cook the noodles in a saucepan of boiling water for 2 minutes, or until tender. Drain, rinse under cold water and cool. Cut into 10 cm (4 inch) lengths.

Put the snow peas in a shallow bowl with the daikon, carrot, spring onion, English spinach leaves and the noodles. Add the dressing and toss. Refrigerate until ready to serve. Just before serving, sprinkle the top with the toasted sesame seeds.

SERVES 4

Vietnamese prawn salad

1 small Chinese cabbage, finely shredded
60 g (2¼ oz/¼ cup) sugar
3 tablespoons fish sauce
4 tablespoons lime juice
1 tablespoon white vinegar
1 small red onion, finely sliced
750 g (1 lb 10 oz) cooked tiger prawns (shrimp), peeled and
    deveined, tails intact
1 small handful coriander (cilantro) leaves, chopped
1 small handful Vietnamese mint leaves, chopped

Put the Chinese cabbage in a large bowl, cover with plastic wrap and chill for 30 minutes.

Put the sugar, fish sauce, lime juice, vinegar and ½ teaspoon salt in a small bowl and mix well.

Toss together the shredded cabbage, onion, sprawns, coriander, mint and dressing, and garnish with the extra mint leaves.

SERVES 6

NOTE: Vietnamese mint is available from Asian markets.

Thai marinated octopus salad

8 baby octopus, cut in half
250 ml (9 fl oz/1 cup) sweet chilli sauce
2 tablespoons lime juice
1 lemon grass stem, trimmed and finely chopped
2 Lebanese (short) cucumbers
50 g (1¾ oz) butter lettuce, torn into rough pieces
50 g (1¾ oz) coriander (cilantro), with stalks

Using a small knife, carefully cut between the head and tentacles of the octopus, just below the eyes. Grasp the body of the octopus and push the beak out with your finger. Cut the eyes from the head of the octopus and discard the eye section. Carefully slit through one side, avoiding the ink sac, and scrape out the gut. Rinse under running water to remove any remaining gut.

Put the octopus in a bowl and add the chilli sauce, lime juice and lemon grass. Stir until well mixed. Cover with plastic wrap and chill for 4 hours.

Cut the cucumbers into 6 cm (2½ inch) lengths, scoop out the seeds and discard. Cut the cucumbers into batons.

Heat a chargrill pan or barbecue hotplate until hot. Remove the octopus from the marinade, reserving the marinade, and cook for 3 minutes, or until cooked through. Cool slightly. Arrange the lettuce and coriander around the edge of a plate, and pile the octopus in the centre.

Add the remaining marinade to the chargrill pan and heat for 2 minutes. Toss the cucumber through the marinade to warm, then spoon over the salad.

SERVES 4

Roasted fennel and orange salad

8 baby fennel bulbs
5 tablespoons olive oil
2 oranges
1 tablespoon lemon juice
1 red onion, halved and thinly
  sliced

100 g (3½ oz) Kalamata olives
2 tablespoons roughly chopped
  mint
1 tablespoon roughly chopped
  flat-leaf (Italian) parsley

Preheat the oven to 200°C (400°F/Gas 6). Trim the fronds from the fennel and reserve. Remove the stalks and cut a slice off the base of each fennel 5 mm (¼ inch) thick. Slice each fennel into 6 wedges, put iin a baking dish and drizzle with 3 tablespoons olive oil. Season well. Bake for 40–45 minutes, or until tender and slightly caramelised. Turn once or twice during cooking. Allow to cool.

Cut a thin slice off the top and bottom of each orange. Using a sharp knife, slice off the skin and pith. Remove as much pith as possible. Slice down the side of a segment between the flesh and the membrane. Repeat with the other side and lift the segment out. Do this over a bowl to catch the juices. Repeat with all the segments on both oranges. Squeeze out any juice remaining in the membranes.

Whisk the remaining oil into the orange juice and the lemon juice until emulsified. Season well. Combine the orange segments, onion and olives in a bowl, pour on half the dressing and add half the mint. Mix well. Transfer to a serving dish. Top with the fennel, drizzle with the remaining dressing, and scatter the parsley and remaining mint over the top. Chop the reserved fronds and sprinkle over the salad.

SERVES 4

mains

Thai beef salad

4 tablespoons lime juice

2 tablespoons fish sauce

2 teaspoons grated palm sugar or soft brown sugar

1 garlic clove, crushed

1 tablespoon finely chopped coriander (cilantro) roots and stems

1 lemon grass stem (white part only), finely chopped

2 small red chillies, finely sliced

2 x 200 g (7 oz) beef eye fillet steaks

150 g (5½ oz) mixed salad leaves

½ red onion, cut into thin wedges

15 g (½ oz) coriander (cilantro) leaves

1 small handful mint leaves, torn

250 g (9 oz) cherry tomatoes, halved

1 Lebanese (short) cucumber, halved lengthways and
    thinly sliced on the diagonal

Mix together the lime juice, fish sauce, palm sugar, garlic, chopped coriander, lemon grass and chilli until the sugar has dissolved.

Preheat the chargrill plate to medium–high direct heat and cook the steaks for 4 minutes on each side, or until medium. Let the steaks cool, then slice thinly across the grain.

Put the salad leaves, onion, coriander leaves, mint, tomatoes and cucumber in a large bowl, add the beef and dressing, toss together and serve immediately.

SERVES 4

Chicken and spinach salad with sesame dressing

450 g (1 lb) baby English spinach leaves
1 Lebanese (short) cucumber, peeled and diced
4 spring onions (scallions), shredded
2 carrots, cut into matchsticks
2 chicken breasts, cooked
2 tablespoons tahini
2 tablespoons lime juice
3 teaspoons sesame oil
1 teaspoon sugar
pinch of chilli flakes
2 tablespoons sesame seeds
1 large handful coriander (cilantro) leaves

Put the spinach in a large bowl. Scatter the cucumber, spring onion and carrot over the top. Shred the chicken breast into long pieces and scatter it over the vegetables.

Mix together the tahini, lime juice, sesame oil, sugar and chilli flakes, then add salt to taste. Drizzle over the salad.

Cook the sesame seeds in a dry frying pan over low heat for 1–2 minutes, stirring, or until starting to brown. Add to the salad. Scatter the coriander leaves over the top. Toss just before serving.

SERVES 4

Tuna and white bean salad

400 g (14 oz) tuna steaks
1 small red onion, thinly sliced
1 tomato, seeded and chopped
1 small red capsicum (pepper), thinly sliced
800 g (1 lb 12 oz) tinned cannellini beans
2 garlic cloves, crushed
1 teaspoon chopped thyme
4 tablespoons finely chopped flat-leaf (Italian) parsley
1½ tablespoons lemon juice
4 tablespoons extra virgin olive oil
1 teaspoon honey
olive oil, for brushing
100 g (3½ oz) rocket (arugula)
1 teaspoon lemon zest

Put the tuna steaks on a plate, sprinkle with cracked black pepper on both sides, cover with plastic wrap and refrigerate until needed.

Combine the onion, tomato and capsicum in a large bowl. Rinse the cannellini beans under cold running water for 30 seconds, drain and add to the bowl with the garlic, thyme and 3 tablespoons of the parsley.

Put the lemon juice, oil and honey in a small saucepan, bring to the boil, then simmer, stirring, for 1 minute, or until the honey dissolves. Remove from the heat.

Brush a chargrill pan or barbecue hotplate with olive oil, and heat until very hot. Cook the tuna for 1 minute on each side. The meat should still be pink in the middle. Slice into 3 cm (1¼ inch) cubes and combine with the salad. Pour on the warm dressing and toss well.

Place the rocket on a platter. Top with the salad, season and garnish with the zest and remaining parsley.

SERVES 4–6

Greek pepper lamb salad

300 g (10½ oz) lamb backstraps
1½ tablespoons cracked black pepper
3 vine-ripened tomatoes, cut into 8 wedges
2 Lebanese (short) cucumbers, sliced
150 g (5½ oz) lemon and garlic marinated Kalamata
   olives, drained (reserving 1½ tablespoons oil)
100 g (3½ oz) feta cheese, cubed
¾ teaspoon dried oregano
1 tablespoon lemon juice
1 tablespoon extra virgin olive oil

Roll the backstraps in the pepper, pressing the pepper on with your fingers. Cover and refrigerate for about 15 minutes. Place the tomato, cucumber, olives, feta and ½ teaspoon of the dried oregano in a bowl.

Heat a chargrill pan or barbecue plate, brush with oil and when very hot, cook the lamb for 2–3 minutes on each side, or until cooked to your liking. Keep warm.

Whisk the lemon juice, extra virgin olive oil, reserved Kalamata oil and the remaining dried oregano together well. Season. Pour half the dressing over the salad, toss together and arrange on a serving platter.

Cut the lamb on the diagonal into 1 cm (½ inch) thick slices and arrange on top of the salad. Pour the rest of the dressing on top and serve.

SERVES 4

Chicken Caesar salad

Caesar dressing
1 egg yolk
1 garlic clove, crushed
3 anchovy fillets
1 teaspoon dijon mustard
125 ml (4 fl oz/½ cup) oil
1 tablespoon lemon juice
½ teaspoon worcestershire
   sauce

15 g (½ oz) grated parmesan
   cheese
4 chicken thigh fillets
4 tablespoons olive oil
12 x 1 cm (½ inch) thick slices
   baguette
1 garlic clove, halved
4 bacon slices
2 baby cos (romaine) lettuces

Put the egg yolk, garlic, anchovies and mustard in a food processor and process. With the motor running, add the oil in a thin stream and process until the mixture is thick. Stir in the lemon juice, worcestershire sauce and parmesan. Season.

Put the chicken thighs in a bowl with 1 tablespoon of olive oil, season to taste and turn to coat well with the oil.

Preheat the chargrill plate to medium–high heat. Brush the baguette slices with the remaining olive oil, and toast on the chargrill plate for 1 minute on each side. Rub both sides of each piece of toast with the cut clove of garlic and keep warm.

Cook the chicken on the chargrill plate for 5 minutes on each side, or until cooked through. Cut into 1 cm (½ inch) strips. Cook the bacon for 3 minutes each side or until crispy, then break it into 2 cm (¾ inch) pieces.

Tear the cos leaves into bite-sized pieces and toss in a large bowl with the dressing, bacon and chicken. Serve with the garlic croutons.

SERVES 4–6

Squid salad with salsa verde

800 g (1 lb 12 oz) squid, scored
and sliced into 4 cm
(1½ inch) diamonds
2 tablespoons olive oil
2 tablespoons lime juice
150 g (5½ oz) green beans
150 g (5½ oz) asparagus spears
1 teaspoon olive oil, extra
100 g (3½ oz) baby rocket
(arugula)

Salsa verde
1 thick slice white bread, crusts
removed
140 ml (5 fl oz) olive oil
3 tablespoons finely chopped
flat-leaf (Italian) parsley
2 teaspoons grated lemon zest
3 tablespoons lemon juice
2 anchovy fillets, finely chopped
2 tablespoons capers, drained
1 garlic clove, crushed

Combine the squid pieces with the olive oil, lime juice and season. Cover with plastic wrap and refrigerate for 2 hours.

To make the salsa verde, break the bread into chunks and drizzle with 2 tablespoons of oil. Put the bread and remaining oil in a food processor with the remaining salsa ingredients, and blend to a paste.

Trim the green beans and asparagus, and cut in half on the diagonal. Blanch the beans for 3 minutes, refresh under cold water, then drain. Blanch the asparagus for 1–2 minutes, refresh in cold water, then drain.

Heat the extra oil in a frying pan over high heat, and cook the marinated squid in batches for 3 minutes per batch, or until cooked. Cool slightly. Combine the green beans, asparagus, rocket and squid. Add 3 tablespoons of the salsa verde and toss. Arrange on a serving platter and drizzle with another tablespoon of salsa verde.

SERVES 4

Spicy lamb and noodle salad

1 tablespoon Chinese five-spice
3 tablespoons vegetable oil
2 garlic cloves, crushed
2 lamb backstraps or fillets
(about 250 g/9 oz each)
500 g (1 lb 2 oz) fresh Shanghai
(wheat) noodles
1½ teaspoons sesame oil
80 g (2¾ oz) snowpea
(mangetout) sprouts
½ red capsicum (pepper), thinly
sliced

4 spring onions (scallions),
thinly sliced on the diagonal
2 tablespoons sesame seeds,
toasted

Dressing
1 tablespoon finely chopped
fresh ginger
1 tablespoon Chinese black
vinegar
1 tablespoon Chinese rice wine
2 tablespoons peanut oil
2 teaspoons chilli oil

Combine the five-spice, 2 tablespoons of the vegetable oil and garlic in a large bowl. Add the lamb and turn to coat well. Cover and marinate for 30 minutes.

Cook the noodles in a saucepan of boiling water for 4–5 minutes, or until tender. Drain, rinse with cold water and drain again. Add the sesame oil and toss.

Heat the remaining vegetable oil in a frying pan. Cook the lamb over medium–high heat for 3 minutes each side for medium–rare. Rest for 5 minutes, then thinly slice across the grain.

To make the dressing, combine the ginger, Chinese black vinegar, rice wine, peanut oil and chilli oil.

Put the noodles, lamb strips, snow pea sprouts, capsicum, spring onion and the dressing in a bowl and toss gently. Sprinkle with the sesame seeds.

SERVES 4

Asian pork salad

2 teaspoons rice vinegar
1 small red chilli, finely chopped
2 tablespoons light soy sauce
1 teaspoon julienned fresh ginger
¼ teaspoon sesame oil
1 star anise
2 teaspoons lime juice
250 g (9 oz) Chinese barbecued pork (char siu)
100 g (3½ oz) snowpea (mangetout) sprouts
2 spring onions (scallions), thinly sliced on the diagonal
½ red capsicum (pepper), thinly sliced

To make the dressing, combine the vinegar, chilli, soy sauce, ginger, sesame oil, star anise and lime juice in a small saucepan. Gently warm for 2 minutes, or until just about to come to the boil, then set aside to cool. Once cool, remove the star anise.

Thinly slice the pork and put in a serving bowl. Pick over the sprouts, discarding any brown or broken ones, and add to the pork. Add the spring onion and capsicum, pour over the dressing and toss well.

SERVES 4

Roasted tomato and pasta salad with pesto

140 ml (5 fl oz) olive oil
500 g (1 lb 2 oz) cherry tomatoes
5 garlic cloves, unpeeled
400 g (14 oz) penne
90 g (3¼ oz/⅓ cup) pesto
3 tablespoons balsamic vinegar
basil leaves, to garnish

Preheat the oven to 180°C (350°F/ Gas 4). Put 2 tablespoons of oil in a roasting dish and place in the oven for 5 minutes. Add the tomatoes and garlic to the dish, season and toss until well coated. Return to the oven and roast for 30 minutes.

Meanwhile, cook the pasta in a large saucepan of rapidly boiling water until *al dente*. Drain and transfer to a large serving bowl.

Squeeze the flesh from the roasted garlic cloves into a bowl. Add the remaining olive oil, the pesto, vinegar and 3 tablespoons of the tomato cooking juices. Season and toss to combine. Add to the pasta and mix well, ensuring that the pasta is coated in the dressing. Gently stir in the cherry tomatoes, then scatter with basil. Serve warm or cold.

SERVES 4

Asian tofu salad

1 large red capsicum (pepper)
1 large green capsicum (pepper)
180 g (6 oz) bean sprouts
4 spring onions (scallions), sliced diagonally
1 small handful coriander (cilantro), chopped
450 g (1 lb) shredded Chinese cabbage
40 g (1½ oz/¼ cup) chopped roasted peanuts
450 g (1 lb) firm tofu
3 tablespoons peanut oil

Dressing
2 tablespoons sweet chilli sauce
2 tablespoons lime juice
½ teaspoon sesame oil
1½ tablespoons light soy sauce
1 garlic clove, finely chopped
3 teaspoons finely grated fresh ginger
3 tablespoons peanut oil

Thinly slice the capsicums, and combine with the bean sprouts, spring onion, coriander, cabbage and peanuts.

Drain the liquid from the tofu and cut into 8 x 2 cm (3 x ¾ inch) wide slices. Heat the oil in a large frying pan. Cook the tofu for 2–3 minutes on each side, or until it is golden with a crispy edge, and add to the salad.

To make the dressing, mix together the chilli sauce, lime juice, oil, soy, garlic and ginger. Whisk in the peanut oil, then toss through the salad and serve immediately.

SERVES 4

Indian marinated chicken salad

3 tablespoons lemon juice
1½ teaspoons garam masala
1 teaspoon ground turmeric
1 tablespoon finely grated fresh
   ginger
2 garlic cloves, finely chopped
3½ tablespoons vegetable oil
3 chicken breast fillets
1 onion, thinly sliced
2 zucchini (courgettes), thinly
   sliced on the diagonal
100 g (3½ oz) watercress leaves

150 g (5½ oz) peas
2 ripe tomatoes, finely chopped
30 g (1 oz) coriander (cilantro)
   leaves

Dressing
1 teaspoon cumin seeds
½ teaspoon coriander seeds
90 g (3¼ oz/⅓ cup) plain
   yoghurt
2 tablespoons chopped mint
2 tablespoons lemon juice

Combine the lemon juice, garam masala, turmeric, ginger, garlic and 2 teaspoons oil in a bowl. Add the chicken and onion. Toss. Cover, and refrigerate for 1 hour.

Remove and discard the onion, then heat 2 tablespoons of oil in a frying pan. Cook the chicken for about 4–5 minutes on each side, or until cooked through. Cut each breast across the grain into 1 cm (½ inch) slices.

Heat the remaining oil in the pan and cook the zucchini for 2 minutes, or until lightly golden. Toss with the watercress in a large bowl. Cook the peas in boiling water for 5 minutes, or until tender, then drain. Rinse under cold water to cool. Add to the salad with the tomato, chicken and coriander.

To make the dressing, roast the cumin and coriander seeds in a dry frying pan for 1–2 minutes, or until fragrant. Remove, then pound the seeds to a powder. Mix with the yoghurt, mint and lemon juice, then fold through the salad.

SERVES 4

Fusilli salad with sherry vinaigrette

300 g (10½ oz) fusilli
250 g (9 oz) cauliflower florets
125 ml (4 fl oz/½ cup) olive oil
16 slices pancetta
10 g (½ oz) small sage leaves
100 g (3½ oz/⅔ cup) pine nuts,
   toasted
2 tablespoons finely chopped
   red Asian shallots
1½ tablespoons sherry vinegar

1 small red chilli, finely chopped
2 garlic cloves, crushed
1 teaspoon soft brown sugar
2 tablespoons orange juice
1 handful flat-leaf (Italian)
   parsley, finely chopped
35 g (1¼ oz/⅓ cup) shaved
   parmesan cheese

Cook the fusilli in a large saucepan of rapidly boiling, salted water for 12 minutes, or until *al dente*. Drain and refresh under cold water until it is cool. Drain well. Blanch the cauliflower florets in boiling water for 3 minutes, then drain and cool.

Heat 1 tablespoon of olive oil in a non-stick frying pan and cook the pancetta for 2 minutes, or until crisp. Drain on crumpled paper towels.

Add 1 tablespoon of oil and cook the sage leaves for 1 minute, or until crisp. Drain on paper towels. In a bowl, combine the pasta, pine nuts and cauliflower.

Heat the remaining olive oil, add the shallots and cook for 2 minutes, or until soft. Remove from the heat then add the vinegar, chilli, garlic, brown sugar, orange juice and parsley. Pour the warm dressing over the pasta and toss to combine.

Place the salad in a serving bowl. Crumble the pancetta over the top and scatter with sage leaves and shaved parmesan. Serve warm.

SERVES 6

Marinated grilled tofu salad

4 tablespoons tamari, shoyu or
   light soy sauce
2 teaspoons oil
2 garlic cloves, crushed
1 teaspoon grated fresh ginger
1 teaspoon chilli paste
500 g (1 lb 2 oz) firm tofu, cut
   into 2 cm (¾ inch) cubes
400 g (14 oz) mixed salad leaves
1 Lebanese (short) cucumber,
   finely sliced

250 g (9 oz) cherry tomatoes,
   halved
2 teaspoons oil, extra

Dressing
2 teaspoons white miso paste
2 tablespoons mirin
1 teaspoon sesame oil
1 teaspoon grated fresh ginger
1 teaspoon finely chopped chives
1 tablespoon toasted sesame
   seeds

Mix together the tamari, oil, garlic, ginger, chilli paste and ½ teaspoon salt. Add the tofu and mix. Marinate for at least 10 minutes. Drain and reserve the marinade.

To make the dressing, combine the miso with 125 ml (4 fl oz/½ cup) of hot water and leave until the miso dissolves. Add the mirin, sesame oil, ginger, chives and sesame seeds and stir thoroughly until it begins to thicken.

Combine the mixed salad leaves, cucumber and tomato in a serving bowl.

Heat the extra oil in a chargrill pan or barbecue hotplate. Add the tofu and cook over medium heat for 4 minutes, or until golden brown. Pour on the reserved marinade and cook for 1 minute over high heat. Remove from the pan and allow to cool for 5 minutes. Add the tofu to the salad, drizzle with the dressing and toss well.

SERVES 4

Beef satay salad

2 teaspoons tamarind pulp
½ teaspoon sesame oil
2 tablespoons soy sauce
2 teaspoons soft brown sugar
2 garlic cloves, crushed
1 tablespoon lime juice
700 g (1 lb 9 oz) rump steak
1 tablespoon peanut oil
6 cos (romaine) lettuce leaves
1 red capsicum (pepper)
180 g (6½ oz) bean sprouts
2 tablespoons fried onion flakes
2 red chillies, chopped
½ teaspoon shrimp paste

1 garlic clove
6 red Asian shallots
2 teaspoons peanut oil
250 ml (9 fl oz/1 cup) coconut milk
1 tablespoon lime juice
120 g (4 oz/¾ cup) unsalted roasted peanuts, finely ground in a food processor
1 tablespoon kecap manis
1 tablespoon soft brown sugar
1 tablespoon fish sauce
2 makrut (kaffir lime) leaves, shredded

Combine the tamarind pulp and 3 tablespoons of boiling water and allow to cool. Mash the pulp to dissolve it, then strain, reserving the liquid. Discard the pulp.

Combine the sesame oil, soy sauce, sugar, garlic, lime juice and 2 tablespoons of tamarind water. Add the steak and cover with plastic wrap. Chill for 2 hours.

Process the chillies, shrimp paste, garlic and shallots to a paste in a food processor. Heat the oil in a frying pan and cook the paste for 3 minutes. Add the coconut milk, lime juice, peanuts, remaining tamarind water, kecap manis, sugar, fish sauce and makrut leaves. Cook until thickened. Thin with 125 ml (4 fl oz/½ cup) of water and return to the boil for 2 minutes. Season. Heat the peanut oil in a frying pan over high heat, and cook the steak for 3 minutes on each side. Slice. Toss the steak slices in a bowl with shredded lettuce, capsicum and the bean sprouts. Drizzle with the sauce and sprinkle with the onion flakes.

SERVES 4

Warm pasta and sweet potato salad

750 g (1 lb 10 oz) orange sweet potato
2 tablespoons extra virgin olive oil
500 g (1 lb 2 oz) casarecci pasta
325 g (11½ oz) marinated feta cheese in oil
3 tablespoons balsamic vinegar
155 g (5½ oz) asparagus, cut into short lengths
100 g (3½ oz) baby rocket (arugula) or baby English spinach leaves
2 vine-ripened tomatoes, chopped
40 g (1½ oz/¼ cup) pine nuts, toasted

Preheat the oven to 200°C (400°F/Gas 6). Peel the sweet potato and cut into large pieces. Put in a baking dish, drizzle with the olive oil and season. Bake for 20 minutes, or until the sweet potato is tender.

Cook the pasta in a large saucepan of rapidly boiling water until *al dente*. Drain well.

Drain the oil from the feta and whisk 3 tablespoons of the oil together with the balsamic vinegar to make a dressing.

Steam the asparagus until bright green and tender. Drain well.

Combine the pasta, sweet potato, asparagus, rocket, feta, tomatoes and pine nuts in a bowl. Add the dressing and toss gently. Season and serve immediately.

SERVES 4

Pepper-crusted salmon salad

1 tablespoon coarsely ground
   black pepper
4 salmon fillets, skin removed
80 g (2¾ oz/⅓ cup) mayonnaise
1½ tablespoons lemon juice
2 teaspoons creamed horseradish
1 small garlic clove, crushed

2 tablespoons chopped flat-leaf
   (Italian) parsley
100 g (3½ oz) watercress
3 tablespoons olive oil
25 g (1 oz) butter
100 g (3½ oz) butter lettuce

Mix the pepper and ¼ teaspoon salt together in a bowl. Coat both sides of each salmon fillet, pressing the pepper down firmly with your fingers. Chill for 30 minutes.

Blend the mayonnaise, lemon juice, horseradish, garlic, parsley, 60 g (2¼ oz) of the watercress, 1 tablespoon of oil and 1 tablespoon of warm water in a food processor for 1 minute. Chill.

Heat the butter and 1 tablespoon oil in a large frying pan until bubbling. Add the salmon fillets and cook over medium–high heat for 2–3 minutes each side, or until cooked to your liking. Remove from the pan and allow to cool slightly.

Wash and dry the butter lettuce, and tear into small pieces. Arrange the lettuce and remaining watercress in the centre of four serving plates, and drizzle lightly with the remaining olive oil. Break each salmon fillet into four or five pieces and arrange over the lettuce. Pour the dressing over the salmon and in a circle around the outside of the leaves.

SERVES 4

Prawn, mango and macadamia salad

1 radicchio heart
25 g (1 oz) basil leaves, torn
30 g (1 oz) watercress sprigs
24 cooked king prawns (shrimp), peeled and
    deveined with tails intact
3 tablespoons macadamia oil
3 tablespoons extra virgin olive oil
150 g (5½ oz/1 cup) macadamia nuts, coarsely chopped
2 garlic cloves, crushed
3 tablespoons lemon juice
1 ripe mango, cut into small dice

Remove the outer green leaves from the radicchio, leaving only the tender pink leaves. Tear any large leaves in half and arrange in a shallow serving bowl. Scatter with half of the basil leaves and the watercress, and toss lightly. Arrange the prawns over the salad leaves.

Heat the oils in a small frying pan over medium heat. Add the nuts and cook for 5 minutes, or until golden. Add the garlic and cook for a further 30 seconds, then remove from the heat and add the lemon juice and mango. Season to taste, pour over the salad and scatter with the remaining basil leaves.

SERVES 4

Warm chicken and pasta salad

375 g (13 oz) penne
100 ml (3½ fl oz) olive oil
4 long, thin eggplants
   (aubergines), thinly sliced on
   the diagonal
2 chicken breast fillets
2 teaspoons lemon juice
15 g (½ oz) flat-leaf (Italian)
   parsley, chopped
270 g (9¾ oz) chargrilled red
   capsicum (pepper), drained
   and sliced

155 g (5½ oz) asparagus spears,
   trimmed, blanched and cut
   into 5 cm (2 inch) lengths
85 g (3 oz) semi-dried
   (sun-blushed) tomatoes,
   finely sliced
grated parmesan cheese,
   (optional)

Cook the pasta in a large saucepan of boiling water until *al dente*. Drain, return to the pan and keep warm.

Heat 2 tablespoons of the oil in a large frying pan over high heat and cook the eggplant for 4–5 minutes, or until golden and cooked through.

Heat a lightly oiled chargrill pan or barbecue hotplate over high heat and cook the chicken for 5 minutes each side, or until browned and cooked through. Cut into thick slices.

Combine the lemon juice, parsley and the remaining oil in a small jar and shake well. Return the pasta to the heat, toss through the dressing, chicken, eggplant, capsicum, asparagus and tomato until well mixed and warmed through. Season with black pepper. Serve warm with grated parmesan, if desired.

SERVES 4

Vietnamese chicken salad

3 chicken breasts or 6 chicken thighs, cooked
2 tablespoons lime juice
1½ tablespoons fish sauce
¼ teaspoon sugar
1–2 bird's eye chillies, finely chopped
1 garlic clove, crushed
2 French shallots, finely sliced
2 handfuls bean sprouts
1 large handful shredded Chinese cabbage
4 tablespoons Vietnamese mint or mint leaves, finely chopped

Take the flesh off the chicken bones and shred it. Discard the skin and bones.

Mix together the lime juice, fish sauce, sugar, chilli, garlic and shallot.

Bring a saucepan of water to the boil and throw in the bean sprouts. After
10 seconds, drain and rinse under cold water to stop them cooking any longer.

Mix the bean sprouts with the Chinese cabbage, Vietnamese mint and chicken.
Pour the dressing over the salad and toss everything together well.

SERVES 4

Seafood salad

500 g (1 lb 2 oz) small squid
1 kg (2 lb 4 oz) large clams
1 kg (2 lb 4 oz) black mussels
500 g (1 lb 2 oz) raw medium prawns (shrimp), peeled, deveined, tails intact
5 tablespoons finely chopped flat-leaf (Italian) parsley

Dressing
2 tablespoons lemon juice
4 tablespoons olive oil
1 garlic clove, crushed

Gently pull apart the body and tentacles of the squid to separate. Remove the head by cutting below the eyes. Push out the beak and discard. Pull the quill from the body of the squid and discard. Under cold running water, pull away all the skin. Rinse well, then slice the squid into rings.

Scrub the clams and mussels and remove the beards. Rinse under running water. Fill a saucepan with 2 cm (¾ inches) of water, add the clams and mussels, cover, and boil for 4–5 minutes. Remove, reserving the liquid. Discard any that do not open. Remove the mussels and clams from their shells and place in a bowl.

Bring 1 litre (35 fl oz/4 cups) water to the boil and add the prawns and squid. Cook for 3–4 minutes, or until the prawns turn pink and the squid is tender. Drain and add to the clams and mussels.

To make the dressing, whisk all of the ingredients together. Season. Pour over the seafood, add 4 tablespoons of the parsley and toss to coat. Cover and refrigerate for 30–40 minutes. Sprinkle with the remaining parsley.

SERVES 4

Chilli chicken and cashew salad

3 tablespoons sweet chilli sauce
2 tablespoons lime juice
2 teaspoons fish sauce
2 tablespoons chopped coriander (cilantro) leaves
1 garlic clove, crushed
1 small red chilli, finely chopped
1½ teaspoons grated fresh ginger
2 tablespoons olive oil
600 g (1 lb 5 oz) chicken breast fillets
100 g (3½ oz) salad leaves
250 g (9 oz) cherry tomatoes, halved
100 g (3½ oz) Lebanese (short) cucumber, cut into bite-sized chunks
50 g (1¾ oz) snowpea (mangetout) sprouts, trimmed
80 g (2¾ oz/½ cup) cashew nuts, roughly chopped

Combine the chilli sauce, lime juice, fish sauce, coriander, garlic, chilli, ginger and 1 tablespoon of the oil in a large bowl.

Heat the remaining oil in a frying pan or chargrill pan over medium heat until hot, and cook the chicken for 5–8 minutes on each side, or until cooked through. Slice each breast widthways into 1 cm (½ inch) slices and toss in the bowl with the dressing. Leave to cool slightly.

Combine the salad leaves, cherry tomatoes, cucumber chunks and snow pea sprouts in a serving bowl. Add the chicken and all of the dressing, and toss gently until the leaves are lightly coated. Scatter with chopped cashews and serve.

SERVES 4

Lamb, capsicum and cucumber salad

1 red onion, very thinly sliced
1 red capsicum (pepper), very thinly sliced
1 green capsicum (pepper), very thinly sliced
2 large Lebanese (short) cucumbers, cut into batons
20 g (¾ oz) shredded mint
3 tablespoons chopped dill
3 tablespoons olive oil
600 g (1 lb 5 oz) lamb backstraps or fillets
4 tablespoons lemon juice
2 small garlic cloves, crushed
100 ml (3½ fl oz) extra virgin olive oil

Combine the onion, red and green capsicum, cucumber, mint and dill in a large bowl.

Heat a chargrill pan or frying pan until hot. Drizzle with the oil and cook the lamb for 2–3 minutes on each side, or until it is tender but still a little pink. Remove from the pan and allow to rest for 5 minutes. Thinly slice the lamb and add to the salad, tossing to mix.

Combine the lemon juice and garlic in a small jug, then whisk in the extra virgin olive oil with a fork until well combined. Season, then gently toss the dressing through the salad.

SERVES 4

Warm prawn, rocket and feta salad

4 spring onions (scallions), chopped
4 Roma (plum) tomatoes, chopped
1 red capsicum (pepper), chopped
400 g (14 oz) tinned chickpeas, drained
1 tablespoon chopped dill
3 tablespoons finely shredded basil
3 tablespoons extra virgin olive oil
60 g (2¼ oz) butter
1 kg (2 lb 4 oz) prawns (shrimp), peeled and deveined, tails intact
2 small red chillies, finely chopped
4 garlic cloves, crushed
2 tablespoons lemon juice
300 g (10½ oz) rocket (arugula)
150 g (5½ oz) feta cheese

Put the spring onion, tomato, capsicum, chickpeas, dill and shredded basil in a large bowl and toss together well.

Heat the oil and butter in a large frying pan or wok, add the prawns and cook, stirring, over high heat for 3 minutes. Add the chilli and garlic and continue cooking for 2 minutes, or until the prawns turn pink. Remove the pan from the heat and stir in the lemon juice.

Arrange the rocket leaves on a large serving platter, top with the tomato and chickpea mixture, then the prawn mixture. Crumble the feta cheese over the top, then serve.

SERVES 4

Minced pork and noodle salad

1 tablespoon peanut oil
500 g (1 lb 2 oz) minced
　(ground) pork
2 garlic cloves, finely chopped
1 lemon grass stem, finely
　chopped
2–3 red Asian shallots, thinly
　sliced
3 teaspoons finely grated fresh
　ginger
1 small red chilli, finely chopped
5 makrut (kaffir lime) leaves,
　very finely shredded
170 g (6 oz) glass (mung bean)
　noodles

60 g (2¼ oz) baby English
　spinach leaves
50 g (1¾ oz) roughly chopped
　coriander (cilantro)
170 g (6 oz) peeled, finely
　chopped fresh pineapple
1 small handful mint leaves

Dressing

1½ tablespoons shaved palm
　sugar or soft brown sugar
2 tablespoons fish sauce
4 tablespoons lime juice
2 teaspoons sesame oil
2 teaspoons peanut oil, extra

Heat a wok until very hot, add the peanut oil and swirl to coat the wok. Add the pork and stir-fry in batches over high heat for 5 minutes, or until lightly golden. Add the garlic, lemon grass, shallots, grated ginger, chilli and lime leaves, and stir-fry for a further 1–2 minutes, or until fragrant.

Place the noodles in a large bowl and cover with boiling water for 30 seconds, or until softened. Rinse under cold water and drain well. Toss in a bowl with the spinach, coriander, pineapple, mint and pork mixture.

To make the dressing, mix together the palm sugar, fish sauce and lime juice. Add the sesame oil and extra peanut oil, and whisk. Toss through the salad and season.

SERVES 4

Roast duck salad with chilli dressing

½ teaspoon chilli flakes
2½ tablespoons fish sauce
1 tablespoon lime juice
2 teaspoons grated palm sugar or soft brown sugar
1 Chinese roasted duck
1 small red onion, thinly sliced
1 tablespoon julienned fresh ginger
20 g (¾ oz) roughly chopped coriander (cilantro)
20 g (¾ oz) roughly chopped mint
80 g (2¾ oz/½ cup) roasted cashews
90 g (3¼ oz) butter lettuce

Put the chilli flakes in a frying pan and dry-fry for 30 seconds, then grind to a powder in a mortar and pestle or spice grinder. Combine the chilli with the fish sauce, lime juice and palm sugar in a bowl, and set aside.

Remove the flesh from the duck and cut it into bite-sized pieces. Place the duck in a bowl with the onion, ginger, coriander, mint and cashews. Pour in the dressing and toss gently.

Place the lettuce on a serving platter. Top with the duck salad and serve.

SERVES 4–6

Thai noodle salad

Dressing
2 tablespoons grated fresh ginger
2 tablespoons soy sauce
2 tablespoons sesame oil
4 tablespoons red wine vinegar
1 tablespoon sweet chilli sauce
2 garlic cloves, crushed
4 tablespoons kecap manis

500 g (1 lb 2 oz) cooked large prawns (shrimp)
250 g (9 oz) dried instant egg noodles
5 spring onions (scallions), sliced diagonally
2 tablespoons chopped coriander (cilantro)
1 red capsicum (pepper), diced
100 g (3½ oz) snow peas (mangetout), sliced

To make the dressing, whisk together the fresh ginger, soy sauce, sesame oil, red wine vinegar, chilli sauce, garlic and kecap manis in a large bowl.

Peel the prawns and gently pull out the dark vein from each prawn back, starting at the head end. Cut each prawn in half lengthways.

Cook the egg noodles in a saucepan of boiling water for 2 minutes, or until tender, then drain thoroughly. Cool in a large bowl.

Add the dressing, prawns and remaining ingredients to the noodles and toss gently. Serve with lime wedges, if desired.

SERVES 4

sides

Baby spinach salad

2 tablespoons olive oil
1 tablespoon lemon juice
150 g (5½ oz) baby English spinach leaves
100 g (3½ oz) small black olives
sea salt, to season

Whisk together the olive oil and the lemon juice.

Toss the spinach in a large serving bowl with the olives and the combined olive oil and lemon juice. Season with sea salt and freshly ground black pepper

SERVES 4

Red potato salad with dill and mustard dressing

6 waxy, red-skinned potatoes (such as desiree)

Dill and mustard dressing
1 tablespoon seeded mustard
1½ tablespoons chopped dill
2 teaspoons soft brown sugar
3 tablespoons red wine vinegar
4 tablespoons olive oil

Steam or boil the potatoes for 20 minutes, or until tender. Remove, and when cool enough to handle, cut into 3 cm (1¼ inch) chunks.

To make the dill and mustard dressing, mix the mustard, dill, brown sugar and vinegar together in a cup. Whisk in the oil with a fork until combined. Toss through the warm potatoes and season.

SERVES 4

Beetroot and chive salad

24 (1.5 kg/3 lb 5 oz) baby beetroot, unpeeled,
 trimmed and washed
50 g (1¾ oz/½ cup) walnut halves
50 g (1¾ oz) roughly chopped watercress
1½ tablespoons snipped chives

Dressing
¼ teaspoon honey
¼ teaspoon dijon mustard
1 tablespoon balsamic vinegar
2 tablespoons olive oil

Preheat the oven to 200°C (400°F/Gas 6). Put the beetroot in a roasting tin, cover with foil and roast for 1 hour, or until tender when pierced with a skewer. Remove from the oven and peel when cool enough to handle.

Meanwhile, to make the dressing, combine the honey, mustard and balsamic vinegar in a cup. Whisk in the oil with a fork until well combined and season.

Reduce the oven temperature to 180°C (350°F/Gas 4). Spread the walnuts on a baking tray and bake for 10 minutes, or until lightly golden. When cool, roughly chop the walnuts.

Combine the watercress, beetroot and chives in a large bowl with the dressing and chopped walnuts and serve.

SERVES 4

Roast tomato salad

6 Roma (plum) tomatoes
2 teaspoons capers, rinsed and drained
6 basil leaves, torn
1 tablespoon olive oil
1 tablespoon balsamic vinegar
2 garlic cloves, crushed
½ teaspoon honey

Cut the tomatoes lengthways into quarters. Place on a baking tray, skin-side down, and cook under a hot grill (broiler) for 4–5 minutes, or until golden. Cool to room temperature and place in a bowl.

Combine the capers, basil leaves, olive oil, balsamic vinegar, crushed garlic and honey in a bowl, season and pour over the tomatoes. Toss gently.

SERVES 6

Chargrilled cauliflower salad

Sesame dressing
3 tablespoons tahini
1 garlic clove, crushed
3 tablespoons seasoned rice
    wine vinegar
1 tablespoon vegetable oil
1 teaspoon lime juice
¼ teaspoon sesame oil

2 tablespoons vegetable oil
2 baby cos (romaine) lettuces
50 g (1¾ oz) picked watercress
    leaves
2 teaspoons sesame seeds,
    toasted
1 tablespoon finely chopped
    flat-leaf (Italian) parsley

1 head cauliflower
12 garlic cloves, crushed

Preheat the chargrill pan or barbecue hotplate to medium heat. In a non-metallic bowl, combine the tahini, garlic, rice wine vinegar, vegetable oil, lime juice, sesame oil and 1 tablespoon water. Whisk together thoroughly and season.

Cut the cauliflower in half, and then into 1 cm (½ inch) wedges. Place on a tray and gently rub with the garlic and vegetable oil. Season well. Chargrill the cauliflower pieces until golden on both sides and cooked through. Remove from the chargrill pan.

Arrange the cos leaves and watercress on a serving platter and top with the chargrilled cauliflower slices. Drizzle the dressing over the top and garnish with the sesame seeds and parsley. Serve immediately.

SERVES 4

Moroccan carrot salad with green olives and mint

1½ teaspoons cumin seeds
½ teaspoon coriander seeds
1 tablespoon red wine vinegar
2 tablespoons olive oil
1 garlic clove, crushed
2 teaspoons harissa
¼ teaspoon orange flower water
600 g (1 lb 5 oz) baby (dutch) carrots, tops trimmed, well scrubbed
40 g (1½ oz/⅓ cup) large green olives, pitted and finely sliced
2 tablespoons shredded mint
30 g (1 oz) picked watercress leaves

In a small frying pan, dry-fry the cumin and coriander seeds for 30 seconds or until fragrant. Cool and then grind in a mortar and pestle or spice grinder. Place into a large mixing bowl with the red wine vinegar, olive oil, garlic, harissa and orange flower water. Whisk to combine.

Blanch the carrots in boiling salted water for 5 minutes, until almost tender. Drain into a colander and allow to sit for a few minutes until they dry. While still hot, add to the red wine vinegar dressing, and toss gently to coat. Allow to cool to room temperature, for the dressing to infuse into the carrots. Add the green olives and mint. Season well and toss gently to combine. Serve on the watercress leaves.

SERVES 4

Minted potato salad

600 g (1 lb 5 oz) chat potatoes, large ones halved
125 g (4½ oz/½ cup) Greek-style yoghurt
1 Lebanese (short) cucumber, grated and squeezed dry
15 g (¼ oz) mint leaves, finely chopped
2 garlic cloves, crushed

Boil or steam the potatoes for 10 minutes, or until tender. Allow to cool.

Mix together the yoghurt, cucumber, mint and garlic and toss through the cooled potatoes. Season well.

SERVES 4

Bean salad

250 g (9 oz) green beans, trimmed
250 g (9 oz) yellow beans, trimmed
3 tablespoons olive oil
1 tablespoon lemon juice
1 garlic clove, crushed
shaved parmesan cheese, to serve

Bring a saucepan of lightly salted water to the boil. Add the green and yellow beans, and cook for 2 minutes, or until just tender. Plunge into cold water and drain.

Put the olive oil, lemon juice and garlic in a bowl, season and mix together well.

Put the beans in a serving bowl, pour on the dressing and toss to coat. Top with the parmesan and serve.

SERVES 6

Snowpea salad with Japanese dressing

250 g (9 oz) snowpeas (mangetout), trimmed
iced water
50 g (1¾ oz) snowpea (mangetout) sprouts
1 small red capsicum (pepper), julienned
½ teaspoon dashi granules
1 tablespoon soy sauce
1 tablespoon mirin
1 teaspoon soft brown sugar
1 garlic clove, crushed
1 teaspoon very finely chopped ginger
¼ teaspoon sesame oil
1 tablespoon vegetable oil
1 tablespoon toasted sesame seeds

Bring a saucepan of water to the boil, add the snowpeas and cook for 1 minute.
Drain, then plunge into a bowl of iced water for 2 minutes. Drain well and
combine with the sprouts and capsicum in a serving bowl.

Dissolve the dashi granules in 1½ tablespoons of hot water and whisk in a small
bowl with the soy sauce, mirin, sugar, garlic, ginger, sesame oil, vegetable oil and
half of the toasted sesame seeds. Pour over the snowpea mixture and toss well.
Season to taste and serve sprinkled with the remaining sesame seeds.

SERVES 4–6

Cucumber salad

1 telegraph (long) cucumber
1 tablespoon sugar
3 tablespoons lime juice
1 tablespoon fish sauce
1 red Asian shallot, finely sliced
10 g (¼ oz) coriander (cilantro) leaves
1 small red chilli, seeds removed and finely chopped
75 g (2½ oz) snowpea (mangetout) shoots

Peel the cucumber, cut in half lengthways, remove the seeds and cut it into 5 mm (¼ inch) slices.

Put the sugar and lime juice in a large bowl, and stir together until the sugar has dissolved, then add the fish sauce.

Toss the cucumber, shallot, coriander and chilli through the dressing, then cover and refrigerate for 15 minutes. Just before serving, cut the snowpea shoots in half and stir through the salad.

SERVES 4

Salata baladi

2 tablespoons extra virgin olive oil
2 tablespoons lemon juice
1 cos (romaine) lettuce, torn into bite-sized pieces
3 ripe tomatoes, each cut into 8 pieces
1 green capsicum (pepper), cut into bite-sized pieces
1 telegraph (long) cucumber, seeded and chopped
6 radishes, sliced
1 small salad or red onion, thinly sliced
2 tablespoons chopped flat-leaf (Italian) parsley
2 tablespoons chopped mint

In a bowl, whisk together the olive oil and lemon juice. Season well.

Combine the vegetables and herbs in a serving bowl and toss well. Add the dressing and toss to combine.

SERVES 4–6

Fennel salad

2 large fennel bulbs
1 tablespoon lemon juice
1 tablespoon extra virgin olive oil
2 teaspoons red wine vinegar
150 g (5½ oz) Niçoise olives, pitted

Trim the fennel bulbs, reserving the fronds, and discard the tough outer layers. Using a very sharp knife, slice the fennel lengthways as thinly as possible and put in a bowl of cold water with the lemon juice.

Just before serving, drain the fennel well and pat dry with paper towels. Toss in a bowl with the olive oil and red wine vinegar. Finely chop the fronds, add them to the fennel with the olives and season to taste.

SERVES 4

Warm potato salad with green olive dressing

1.5 kg (3 lb 5 oz) nicola potatoes, scrubbed
  (or any small, waxy potato)
90 g (3¼ oz/½ cup) green olives, pitted and finely chopped
2 teaspoons capers, finely chopped
15 g (¼ oz) flat-leaf (Italian) parsley, finely chopped
2 tablespoons lemon juice
1 teaspoon finely grated lemon zest
2 garlic cloves, crushed
125 ml (4 fl oz/½ cup) extra virgin olive oil

Boil the potatoes for 15 minutes or until just tender (pierce with the tip of a sharp knife—if the potato comes away easily it is ready). Drain and cool slightly.

Meanwhile, place the olives and capers in a small bowl with the parsley, lemon juice, lemon zest, garlic and olive oil. Whisk with a fork to combine.

Cut the potatoes into halves and gently toss with the dressing while still warm. Season to taste.

SERVES 6

Warm artichoke salad

8 young globe artichokes
(200 g/7 oz each)
1 lemon
25 g (1 oz) shredded basil
50 g (1¾ oz/½ cup) shaved
parmesan cheese

Dressing
1 garlic clove, finely chopped
½ teaspoon sugar
1 teaspoon dijon mustard
2 teaspoons finely chopped
lemon zest
3 tablespoons lemon juice
4 tablespoons extra virgin olive
oil

Remove the tough outer leaves from the artichokes until you get to the pale green leaves. Cut across the top of the artichoke, halfway down the tough leaves, then trim the stems to 4 cm (1½ inches) long, and lightly peel them. Cut each artichoke in half lengthways and remove the hairy choke with a teaspoon. Rub each artichoke with lemon while you work and place in a bowl of cold water mixed with lemon juice to prevent the artichokes from turning brown.

Place the artichokes in a large saucepan of boiling water, top with a plate or heatproof bowl to keep them immersed, and cook for 25 minutes, or until tender. To check tenderness, place a skewer into the largest part of the artichoke. It should insert easily. Drain and cut in half again to serve.

For the dressing, mix the garlic, sugar, mustard, lemon zest and lemon juice in a cup. Season, then whisk in the oil with a fork until combined. Pour over the artichoke and scatter with the basil and parmesan.

SERVES 4

Cherry and pear tomato salad with white beans

3 tablespoons olive oil
2 red Asian shallots, finely diced
1 large garlic clove, crushed
1½ tablespoons lemon juice
250 g (9 oz) red cherry tomatoes, halved
250 g (9 oz) yellow pear tomatoes, halved
425 g (15 oz) tinned white beans, drained and rinsed
20 g (¾ oz) basil leaves, torn
2 tablespoons chopped flat-leaf (Italian) parsley

Put the olive oil, diced shallots, crushed garlic and lemon juice into a small bowl and whisk to combine.

Put the halved cherry and pear tomatoes and the white beans in a serving bowl. Drizzle with the dressing and scatter the basil and parsley over the top. Toss gently to combine.

SERVES 4

Asian salad

2 sheets nori, cut into 3 cm x 5 mm (1¼ x ¼ inch) pieces
2 tablespoons seasoned rice wine vinegar
2 teaspoons lemon juice
¼ teaspoon sesame oil
2 teaspoons canola oil
60 g (2¼ oz) mizuna leaves
60 g (2¼ oz) snowpea (mangetout) shoots
2 Lebanese (short) cucumbers, shaved
½ daikon, shaved

Toast the nori on a preheated barbecue plate for 5 minutes, or until crispy.

To make the dressing, whisk together the vinegar, lemon juice, sesame oil and canola oil. Toss the mizuna, snowpea shoots, cucumber, daikon and nori with the dressing and serve.

SERVES 4

Thai green papaya salad

500 g (1 lb 2 oz) green papaya, peeled and seeded
1–2 small red chillies, thinly sliced
1 tablespoon grated palm sugar
1 tablespoon soy sauce
2 tablespoons lime juice
1 tablespoon fried garlic (see Note)
1 tablespoon fried shallots (see Note)
50 g (1¾ oz) green beans, cut into 1 cm (½ inch) lengths
8 cherry tomatoes, quartered
2 tablespoons chopped roasted unsalted peanuts

Grate the papaya into long, fine shreds with a zester or a knife.

Place the papaya in a large mortar and pestle with the chilli, palm sugar, soy sauce and lime juice. Lightly pound until combined. Add the fried garlic and shallots, beans and tomatoes. Lightly pound for a further minute, or until combined. Serve immediately, sprinkled with the peanuts.

SERVES 4

NOTE: Packets of fried garlic and shallots are available from Asian food stores.

Radicchio with figs and ginger vinaigrette

1 radicchio
1 small curly endive lettuce (see Note)
3 oranges
½ small red onion, thinly sliced into rings
8 small green figs, quartered
3 tablespoons extra virgin olive oil
1 teaspoon red wine vinegar
⅛ teaspoon ground cinnamon
2 tablespoons orange juice
2 tablespoons very finely chopped glacé ginger with syrup
2 pomegranates (optional)

Wash the radicchio and curly endive leaves in cold water and drain well. Tear any large leaves into pieces.

Peel and segment the oranges, discarding all of the pith. Place in a large bowl with the onion rings, salad leaves and figs, reserving 8 fig quarters.

Combine the olive oil, vinegar, cinnamon, orange juice and ginger in a small cup. Season to tast. Pour over the salad and toss lightly.

Arrange the reserved figs in pairs over the salad. If you are using the pomegranates, slice in half and scoop out the seeds with a spoon. Scatter over the salad.

SERVES 4

Cucumber, feta, mint and dill salad

120 g (4 oz) feta cheese
4 Lebanese (short) cucumbers
1 small red onion, thinly sliced
1½ tablespoons finely chopped dill
1 tablespoon dried mint
3 tablespoons olive oil
1½ tablespoons lemon juice

Crumble the feta into 1 cm (½ inch) pieces and put in a large bowl.

Peel and seed the cucumbers and cut into 1 cm (½ inch) dice. Add to the bowl along with the onion and dill.

Grind the mint in a mortar and pestle until powdered. Combine with the oil and juice, then season. Pour over the salad and toss well.

SERVES 4

Warm marinated mushroom salad

750 g (1 lb 10 oz) mixed mushrooms (such as baby button, oyster,
   Swiss brown, shiitake and enoki)
2 garlic cloves, finely chopped
½ teaspoon green peppercorns, crushed
4 tablespoons olive oil
4 tablespoons orange juice
250 g (9 oz) salad leaves, watercress or baby spinach leaves
1 teaspoon finely grated orange zest

Trim the mushroom stems and wipe the mushrooms with a damp paper towel.
Cut any large mushrooms in half. Mix together the garlic, peppercorns, olive oil
and orange juice. Pour over the mushrooms and marinate for about 20 minutes.

Arrange the salad leaves in a large serving dish.

Drain the mushrooms, reserving the marinade. Cook the flat and button
mushrooms on a hot, lightly oiled barbecue grill or flat plate for about 2 minutes.
Add the softer mushrooms and cook for 1 minute, or until they just soften.

Scatter the mushrooms over the salad leaves and drizzle with the marinade.
Sprinkle with orange zest and season well.

SERVES 4

Warm choy sum salad

370 g (13 oz) choy sum
2 tablespoons peanut oil
3 teaspoons finely grated ginger
2 garlic cloves, finely chopped
2 teaspoons sugar
2 teaspoons sesame oil
2 tablespoons soy sauce
1 tablespoon lemon juice
2 teaspoons seasame seeds, toasted

Trim the ends from the choy sum and slice in half. Steam for 2 minutes or until wilted and arrange on a serving plate.

Heat a small saucepan until very hot, add the peanut oil and swirl it around to coat the pan. Add the ginger and garlic and stir-fry for 1 minute. Add the sugar, sesame oil, soy sauce and lemon juice, heat until hot and pour over the choy sum. Season to taste, garnish with sesame seeds and serve immediately.

SERVES 4

Lentil salad

½ brown onion
2 cloves
300 g (10½ oz/1⅔ cups) puy lentils (see Note)
1 strip lemon zest
2 garlic cloves, peeled
1 fresh bay leaf
2 teaspoons ground cumin
2 tablespoons red wine vinegar
3 tablespoons olive oil
1 tablespoon lemon juice
2 tablespoons finely chopped mint leaves
3 spring onions (scallions), finely chopped

Stud the onion with the cloves and place in a saucepan with the lentils, zest, garlic, bay leaf, 1 teaspoon cumin and 875 ml (30 fl oz/3½ cups) of water. Bring to the boil and cook over medium heat for 25–30 minutes, or until the water has been absorbed. Discard the onion, zest and bay leaf. Reserve the garlic and finely chop.

Whisk together the vinegar, oil, juice, garlic and remaining cumin. Stir through the lentils with the mint and spring onion. Season well. Leave for 30 minutes to let the flavours absorb. Serve at room temperature.

SERVES 4–6

NOTE: Puy lentils are small, green lentils from France. They are available dried from gourmet food stores.

Eggplant, tomato and sumac salad

2 eggplants (aubergines), cut into 1 cm (½ inch) thick rounds
100 ml (3½ fl oz) olive oil
5 large ripe tomatoes
1 small red onion, finely sliced
20 g (¾ oz) mint leaves, roughly chopped
10 g (¼ oz) flat-leaf (Italian) parsley, roughly chopped
2 teaspoons sumac (see Note)
2 tablespoons lemon juice

Put the eggplant slices in a colander, and sprinkle with salt. Leave the eggplant for 30 minutes to allow some of the bitter juices to drain away, then rinse the slices and pat them dry with paper towels. Using 2 tablespoons of the olive oil, brush both sides of each slice, then chargrill for 5 minutes on each side or until they are cooked through. Let the slices cool slightly and cut them in half.

Cut the tomatoes into wedges and arrange in a serving bowl with the eggplant and onion. Scatter the mint, parsley and sumac over the top.

Put the lemon juice and remaining olive oil in a screw-top jar, season and shake. Drizzle the dressing over the salad and toss gently.

SERVES 6

NOTE: Sumac is a spice made from crushing the dried sumac berry. It has a mild lemony flavour and is used extensively in many cuisines, from North Africa and the Middle East, to India and Asia.

Chickpea salad

800 g (1 lb 12 oz) tinned chickpeas
3 tomatoes
1 red onion, thinly sliced
1 small red capsicum (pepper), cut into thin strips
4 spring onions (scallions), cut into thin strips
60 g (2¼ oz) flat-leaf (Italian) parsley, chopped
2–3 tablespoons chopped mint leaves

Dressing
2 tablespoons tahini
2 tablespoons lemon juice
3 tablespoons olive oil
2 garlic cloves, crushed
½ teaspoon ground cumin

Drain the chickpeas and rinse well. Cut the tomatoes in half and remove the seeds with a spoon. Dice the flesh. Mix the red onion, tomato, capsicum and spring onion in a bowl. Add the chickpeas, parsley and mint.

To make the dressing, put all the ingredients in a screw-top jar with 2 tablespoons of water, season well and shake. Pour over the salad and toss.

SERVES 8

Asian rice salad

400 g (14 oz/2 cups) long-grain rice
2 tablespoons olive oil
1 large red onion, finely chopped
4 garlic cloves, crushed
1 tablespoon finely chopped fresh ginger
1 long red chilli, seeded and thinly sliced
4 spring onions (scallions), finely sliced
2 tablespoons soy sauce
½ teaspoon sesame oil
2 teaspoons black vinegar (see Note)
1 tablespoon lime juice
50 g (1¾ oz) roughly chopped coriander (cilantro) leaves

Bring 1.25 litres (44 fl oz/5 cups) of water to the boil in a large saucepan. Add the rice and cook it, uncovered, for 12–15 minutes over low heat, or until the grains are tender. Drain and rinse the rice under cold running water, then transfer to a large bowl.

While the rice is cooking, heat the oil in a frying pan over medium heat. Add the onion, garlic, ginger and chilli, and cook them for 5–6 minutes, or until the onion has softened, but not browned. Stir in the spring onion and cook for another minute. Remove the onion mixture from the heat and add it to the rice with the soy sauce, sesame oil, vinegar, lime juice and coriander, and mix well. Cover the rice salad and refrigerate until you are ready to serve.

SERVES 4

NOTE: Black vinegar is a type of Chinese vinegar and can be found in Asian grocery stores.

Caramelised onion and potato salad

oil, for cooking
6 red onions, thinly sliced
1 kg (2 lb 4 oz) Kipfler or new potatoes, unpeeled
4 bacon slices
30 g (1 oz) chives, snipped

Mayonnaise
250 g (9 oz/1 cup) whole-egg mayonnaise
1 tablespoon dijon mustard
juice of 1 lemon
2 tablespoons sour cream

Heat 2 tablespoons of oil in a large heavy-based frying pan, add the onion and cook over medium–low heat for 40 minutes, or until soft and caramelised.

Cut the potatoes into large chunks. Cook in boiling water for 10 minutes, or until just tender, then drain and cool slightly.

Grill (broil) the bacon until crisp. Drain on paper towels and cool slightly before chopping.

Put the potato, onion and chives in a large bowl, reserving a few chives to garnish, and mix well.

To make the mayonnaise, put the whole-egg mayonnaise, mustard, lemon juice and sour cream in a bowl and whisk to combine. Pour over the salad and toss to coat. Sprinkle with the bacon and garnish with the reserved chives.

SERVES 10

index

First published in 2008 by Murdoch Books Pty Limited

Murdoch Books Australia
Pier 8/9, 23 Hickson Road
Millers Point NSW 2000
Phone: +61 (0) 2 8220 2000
Fax: +61 (0) 2 8220 2558
www.murdochbooks.com.au

Murdoch Books UK Limited
Erico House, 6th Floor
93–99 Upper Richmond Road,
Putney, London SW15 2TG
Phone: +44 (0) 20 8785 5995
Fax: +44 (0) 20 8785 5985
www.murdochbooks.co.uk

Chief Executive: Juliet Rogers
Publishing Director: Kay Scarlett

Design Manager: Vivien Valk
Project manager and editor: Gordana Trifunovic
Design concept: Alex Frampton
Designer: Susanne Geppert
Production: Monique Layt
Cover photography: Tanya Zouev
Styling: Stephanie Souvlis
Introduction text: Leanne Kitchen
Recipes developed by the Murdoch Books Test Kitchen

Printed by Sing Cheong Printing Co. Ltd in 2008. PRINTED IN HONG KONG.

ISBN 9781741961164 (pbk.).
A catalogue record for this book is available from the British Library.

IMPORTANT: Those who might be at risk from the effects of salmonella poisoning (the elderly, pregnant women, young children and those suffering from immune deficiency diseases) should consult their doctor with any concerns about eating raw eggs.

CONVERSION GUIDE: You may find cooking times vary depending on the oven you are using. For fan-forced ovens, as a general rule, set the oven temperature to 20°C (35°F) lower than indicated in the recipe. We have used 20 ml (4 teaspoon) tablespoon measures. If you are using a 15 ml (3 teaspoon) tablespoon, for most recipes the difference will not be noticeable. However, for recipes using baking powder, gelatine, bicarbonate of soda (baking soda), small amounts of flour and cornflour (cornstarch), add an extra teaspoon for each tablespoon specified.